"Hey God, can I ask you something?"
Bible based answers for questions asked by kids.

By Brad R. Emery
[Copyright © Brad R. Emery, 2024]
Illustrations by Tiarne Hookham
Soul Window Books
An imprint of Opensight Communications
Edited by Rev. Matt Johnson, South Sydney Anglican Church
ISBN – 978-0-646-89434-8
BISG REL091000

For Willow.

Contents

Foreward **4**

-1-   Hey God, who are you really? **5**

-2-   God, did you really create people, ... **10**
      the world, the galaxy and everything?

-3-   Dear God, how can I be sure the Bible **16**
      is really true and accurate?

-4-   Excuse me God, was Jesus just make believe **20**
      or was he a real person?

-5-   Hey God, if Jesus was so great why did he **23**
      let himself be killed?

-6-   Dear God, did Jesus really rise from the dead? ... **27**

-7-   Why can't I see you, God? **34**

-8-	Hey God, can you really do anything?	**37**
-9-	Hey God, how do I talk to you?	**39**
-10-	How can I be sure you love me, God?	**42**
-11-	Dear God, if you love us, why do bad and sad things still happen?	**46**
-12-	Um, God, what if I'm scared of dying?	**48**
-13-	So, God, why should I obey you?	**51**
-14-	Hey God, what should I say to my friends who don't believe you are real?	**53**
Conclusion		**56**
References		**58**
About the Author		**59**

Foreword

If you could ask God a question, what would it be?

You may have been reading the Bible since you were very little, or maybe you're just starting to look into the Bible and finding out what it says about God and how much He loves us.

As we read the Bible and learn more about God, questions often pop up about what we discover. Big questions, sometimes hard questions about God, Jesus, the natural world, and even the Bible itself. Sometimes we wish we could just ask God Himself some of these difficult questions.

What's awesome is that God answers many of the questions we might have through His word, the Bible.

In fact, the reason for writing this book is that from a young age, my own daughter would ask me some of the tough questions that jump out of the pages of the Bible.

Like 99.9 per cent of people, I'm a parent and not a church pastor or minister, so the aim of this book is to provide helpful answers to some of these questions from the Bible and from those who have studied God's word.

It may not answer every question you've ever had, but it will help with some of the really important ones.

I pray you find it useful.

Brad R. Emery

With thanks to: Reverend Matthew Johnson for his input, Renee Emery for her wisdom and Scott Monk for his tutelage.

- 1 -
Hey God, who are you really?

When we meet someone new, we might say 'Hi there, what's your name?' Then we start to find out about them; where they are from and the sort of things they like. The more time we spend with them, the more we get to know them.

What's awesome is that God doesn't hide Himself from us. In the Bible God reveals to us who He is, what He's like and what He thinks about us.

Firstly, the Bible tells us that God is one spiritual Being who existed before time and creation began. No one made God. He had no mum or dad. God has always existed and always will. In the book of Revelation chapter 1 verse 8 God Himself says "'I am the Alpha and the Omega,' says the Lord God, 'who is, and who was, and who is to come, the Almighty.'"

In the Greek alphabet, Alpha is the very first letter and Omega is the very last letter. So, God is telling us that He existed at the beginning and will still exist at the end.

The Bible also tells us that God is absolutely holy. That means God is perfect and distinct from everything else in creation. God's holiness means that He is without sin and absolutely pure.

God also reveals to us that He is unchanging. The Bible tells us that He is exactly the same loving God today as He was before time began.

In the book of Malachi in the Old Testament, chapter 3 verse 6 God tells his people, "For I, the LORD, do not change..."

Again, in the New Testament - hundreds of years later - one of Jesus' disciples James wrote in James chapter 1 verse 17, "Every good and perfect gift is from above, coming down from the Father of the heavenly lights, who does not change like shifting shadows."

God has also revealed that He is everywhere at once. Yep, He's that powerful! Bible teachers call this being 'omnipresent'. For us it means God can listen to the prayer of a girl in Chicago, USA and watch over a boy in Abuja, Nigeria at the same time!

There is nowhere we can go where God will not be with us; nowhere where we can go that we cannot talk to Him.

In the book of Psalms chapter 139 verses 7 and 8 the writer says,

"Where can I go from your Spirit?

Where can I flee from your presence?

If I go up to the heavens, you are there;

if I make my bed in the depths, you are there."

God is always with us, no matter how lost we sometimes feel.

The Bible also tells us that God is all knowing. Bible teachers call this 'omniscient'. Some people love football. They love it so much they know the name and statistics for every player on their favourite team.

That's nothing compared to God! There is absolutely nothing God does not know about you, me, everything and everyone. Again, in Psalm 139 verses 1 to 4 the writer says:

"You have searched me, LORD,
   and you know me.
You know when I sit and when I rise;
   you perceive my thoughts from afar.
You discern my going out and my lying down;
   you are familiar with all my ways.
Before a word is on my tongue
   you, LORD, know it completely."

Hundreds of years later, in the Gospel of Matthew chapter 10, Jesus told his followers not to worry or be afraid because God knows everything, telling them "Even the very hairs of your head are all numbered."

The most special aspect of God for you and me is that the Bible tells us God is 'love' and that He lavishes that love upon us!

In the New Testament book of 1 John chapter 4 verse 8, Jesus' disciple John writes:

"Whoever does not love does not know God, because God is love."

To say God is love is to say that He is good, gracious and overflowing in mercy. He showed us just how much He is love by sending His Son Jesus to take the penalty that we were meant to pay, once for all time by dying on the cross.

By doing so, God made us His children! John tells us this in 1 John chapter 3 verse 1. "See what great love the Father has lavished on us, that we should be called children of God! And that is what we are!"

God loves us as His precious children!

So, God is all knowing, all powerful, is everywhere at once and loves us as his own. Isn't that incredible?

Did you know...

Did you know the Indigenous Australians of the Yankunytjatjara Nation in Central Australia have a word Kanyini which has a very deep and special meaning? Kanyini means connectedness to every other living thing, especially the connection to tjukurrpa, knowledge of creation or 'Dreaming'; ngura, which means 'place'; walytja, 'family'; and kurunpa which means 'spirit' or 'soul'. Kanyini is the connection expressed by looking after all other living things around you[1].

And did you know the ancient Greeks had seven words for love? All of them were words to describe the types of love humans experience with each other. Then there was one special one – Agape. That's the word for God's love which is unique and perfect, not tainted by sin or our selfish motives. It's the merciful, blessed, gracious love God has for you and me!

- 2 -
God, did you really create people, the world, the galaxy and everything?

The book of Genesis tells us that God made the world, the universe and everything in it. He did so by speaking powerful words. With these words, everything came into being – lions and lizards, sandy beaches and snowy mountains, and of course people – God did it all.

The Bible doesn't tell us exactly how God created everything. It simply says that he spoke and creation began, starting with Genesis chapter 1, verse 3 "And God said, 'let there be light' and there was light." In the New Testament, the book of Hebrews chapter 11, verse 3 goes on to say, "By faith we understand that the universe was formed at God's command, so that what is seen was not made out of what was visible." Isn't that amazing?

However, God did give us the gift of science so we could catch a small glimpse of His design, that is, how the universe and all living things are put together. Science can help us see the order, purpose and wisdom with which God created everything. Through science we can look at enormous things like what the stars in the night sky are made of and how deep the deepest part of the Pacific Ocean is, all the way down to how tiny blood cells are formed inside our bodies.

And there are many scientists who believe that all of creation points to a 'creator' – to God. Famous astronomer, Dr Allan Sandage, once wrote that he found it 'quite improbable' that the order found in creation came out of 'chaos' – in other words, creation didn't all just happen by accident. In fact, Dr Sandage believed that God was the "explanation for the miracle of existence."[1]

Did you know...

Did you know lots of scientists believe there is a God? In 2009 a survey of scientists in America found that just over half of scientists (51%) believe in some form of deity or higher power. Specifically, 33% say they believe in God.[2] One of these scientists has studied human beings more closely than probably anyone else. Dr Francis Collins led the Human Genome Project, an international study that mapped all 3.1 billion base pairs in human DNA. DNA is like the blueprint of what makes us human.

For most of his life, Dr Collins didn't believe there was a God. Later in his career, Dr Collins realised "I had done something that a scientist is not supposed to do: I had drawn a conclusion without looking at the data."[3] After investigating all the evidence about God, Dr Collins came to believe that the God of the Bible was really true and became a Christian – "Everything I do as a scientist reinforces my sense of God's presence because every new discovery is, if you believe in his role as creator, a glimpse into His mind. And I find that very meaningful and satisfying to be able to have the experience of discovery by both the natural world unveiling itself and also getting a glimpse into what God's plan was."

- 3 -
Dear God, how can I be sure the Bible is really true and accurate?

If your grandma or grandpa sent you a birthday present in the post, you would know it came from them because they wrote the card themselves.

In a similar way we can be confident the Bible is true because it comes from God Himself. In the book of 2 Timothy, chapter 3 verses 16 and 17, the Apostle Paul tells Timothy that "All Scripture is God-breathed and is useful for teaching, rebuking, correcting and training in righteousness, so that the servant of God may be thoroughly equipped for every good work."

God didn't write the Bible with pen and paper like we use. Instead, over the centuries, God spoke to people He chose, who then wrote down His word. These included kings, a doctor, a prince, a shepherd, a tax collector, a fisherman and specially gifted religious leaders called prophets. They all recorded God's word so that everyone, including us, could learn from it.

In the book of 2 Peter, chapter 1 verses 20 and 21, the Apostle Peter tells us "Above all, you must understand that no prophecy of Scripture came about by the prophet's own interpretation of things. For prophecy never had its origin in the human will, but prophets, though human, spoke from God as they were carried along by the Holy Spirit."

You see from the beginning of the Bible, God was showing His servants exactly what needed to be written to form the Holy Bible we have today.

We can also trust the Bible because it records the life of Jesus himself and the prophesies about him from the Old Testament. In the book of Micah chapter 5 verse 2, the prophet Micah tells God's people that God's saviour would be born in the town of Bethlehem – that's exactly where Jesus was born!

In the book of Isaiah chapter 53, the prophet Isaiah says that God's saviour would be "pierced for our transgressions" and that "the punishment that brought us peace was upon him and by his wounds we are healed." This was written 700 years before Jesus was born but described exactly what happened to him when he died on the cross. God was guiding His prophets in the Old Testament on what was going to happen to Jesus hundreds of years later and it all happened exactly the way He said it would!

There's also other evidence that we can look at to give us confidence that the Bible is as accurate today as when it was first written.

For example, while none of the original copies of the New Testament exists, we have thousands of ancient copies and fragments of the New Testament. Many of these were copied very close to when the original books were written and almost every single piece of text is true to the original.

The earliest complete copies of the New Testament date between 300-325AD. Significant portions of the New Testament, including parts of John's Gospel, Paul's letters and the book of Hebrews date back to 200AD. There are even fragments going all the way back to around the time of Roman Emperor Hadrian, 117-138AD. That's very close to when the original manuscripts of the New Testament were actually written.[1]

As far as historical accuracy goes, the New Testament is by far the best certified document from the ancient world!

Did you know...

Did you know that the oldest surviving copies of most ancient texts were copied more than 700 years after the original document was written?[2]. For example, Julius Caesar wrote about his war in Gaul – today we call it France – in the first century B.C. The oldest copy we have was written down 900 years later![3] Not so with the Bible. In the John Rylands Library in the United Kingdom, there is a fragment of the Gospel of John that dates to within just 40 years of when it was originally written.[4] There's also a near complete copy of the New Testament in the Chester Beatty Library in Ireland that was copied only around 150 years after it was first written![5]

- 4 -
Excuse me God, was Jesus just make believe or was he a real person?

Jesus sure was a real person.

In the Bible, the accounts of Jesus – called Gospels – were written by two of his disciples, Matthew and John, one of his other followers, Mark and the fourth by a doctor and historian named Luke. The Gospels tell us that Jesus was born in Bethlehem, grew up in Nazareth with his parents and started preaching about God when he was in his thirties.

The Gospel of Luke is a really good place to learn about Jesus. Luke was a well-educated man, who researched everything he could to put together an accurate account of Jesus's birth, his life as a boy and his teachings.

BIRTH OF
Jesus

That's why Luke starts his account by telling us that Jesus was born around the same time that Herod was the King of Judea and that Caesar Augustus was the Emperor of Rome. That's like your parents telling you who the President or Prime Minister was when you were born. Luke wanted us to know that Jesus was born at a specific point in history, and we can cross-check that with other ancient history books.

It's not only the Bible that tells us that Jesus was a real historical person. Other people who lived around the same time as Jesus wrote about him in ancient documents that have survived to this day.

Josephus was a Jewish historian who wrote about Jesus. Tacitus was a Roman historian who wrote about 'the Christ'. And there's a collection of Jewish writings called the Babylonian Talmud, which also mention that Jesus was crucified on the cross.[1]

These first two authors were considered to be two of the most famous historians of their time. These ancient writings outside of the Bible help us confirm that Jesus really was a person in history.

Did you know...

Did you know that well-known experts in ancient history from around the world agree that Jesus was a real person? Ed Sanders from Duke University in the USA[2] has studied the history of Jesus for almost forty years; Christopher Tuckett from the University of Oxford in England[3] contributed to a university textbook about Jesus; and Gerd Thiessen from Germany is a leading expert on the history of Jesus.[4] All three of these experts agree that the Jesus we read about in the Bible really did exist!

- 5 -
Hey God, if Jesus was so great why did he let himself be killed?

Did you know that there are only a handful of animals in the world that cannot walk backwards? Even more peculiar is at least two of them both come from the same country!

No matter how hard they try, the Kangaroo and Emu, both from Australia, are two animals that simply can't walk backwards.

That's kind of like us. The Bible tells us that no matter how hard we try, we can never live up to the perfect holiness that our Holy God requires. God is supremely perfect and supremely holy, which means He cannot be in the presence of sin.

That's bad news for everyone who has ever lived as both the Old and New Testaments tell us: "As it is written: There is no one righteous, not even one;... there is no one who does good, not even one." (Romans 3:10-12)

Because we're 'unrighteous' - or separate from God – the punishment is death. You see when sin and evil entered the world, it tainted everything, including human beings. Forever. It means from the moment we're born, the taint of sin is upon us. Since God is perfectly pure and holy, He cannot be in the presence of sin.

The only way for people to be right with God was for a price to be paid for their sins and the only price for sin is death. In the Old Testament, this required God's priests to sacrifice animals for the sins of the people. However, this wasn't the way God wanted it, as sacrifices had to be made over and over to make His people right with Him.

But God had a plan. The Bible tells us that because God loves us so much, He put in place a plan for our penalty to be paid. Forever. He chose to pay that price of death Himself by sending His only perfect Son, Jesus, to die on the cross. Jesus took the punishment for all who believe in him, once for all time. Can you imagine how much Jesus must love you to have taken that penalty for you? Through this we have 'forever' peace with God, and can call Him our Father.

In the Gospel of John chapter 3 verse 16, we're told exactly why Jesus died. "For God so loved the world, that he gave his one and only Son that whoever believes in him should not perish but have eternal life."

That promise is for YOU if you believe in Jesus!

Did you know...

Did you know that the Apostle Paul wrote that he was at the top of the class when it came to following the Laws God had given His people through Moses? In the book of Philippians chapter 3, Paul writes that he was the best-of-the-best when it came to doing the right thing and obeying all the rules. And yet Paul writes that all of this could not make him right with God. Paul describes all his so-called 'goodness' as rubbish compared to having faith in Jesus and in his death and resurrection for us!

- 6 -
Dear God, did Jesus really rise from the dead?

He sure did. In fact, Jesus rising from the dead is at the heart of what it means to be a Christian. The resurrection shows how much God loves us and gives us hope that one day we will live with Him forever.

As we've already talked about, Gospel writer Luke was a doctor and also the first 'Bible historian'. Luke wanted to make sure people had accurate evidence that Jesus rose from the dead.

Before writing his account of Jesus' resurrection, Luke spoke to as many people as he could who had seen the resurrected Jesus. In Luke chapter 24, he writes that on one occasion after he rose from the dead, Jesus appeared to all his disciples at once. At first they thought he was a ghost! So, Jesus invited them to touch his hands where the nails had pierced him on the cross. He even asked them for something to eat to show them he was alive!

The Apostle Paul wrote in 1 Corinthians chapter 15 that Jesus also appeared to more than 500 people! That's a lot of witnesses, many of whom were still alive when Paul wrote this letter to the church in Corinth.

There's also logical evidence we can follow to support what the Bible says about Jesus rising from the dead.

Jesus wasn't buried somewhere secret. The Bible tells us that everyone knew Jesus was buried in the personal tomb of a wealthy and well-known man called Joseph of Arimathea. The Jewish leaders knew where the tomb was because they sent soldiers to guard it. Jesus' followers knew where the tomb was because they went to the tomb early on the third day to put sweet smelling spices on Jesus' body.

Dr John Lennox, a Professor at Oxford University in England, therefore, argues that if Jesus' tomb was not empty on the third day after he died, as the disciples claimed, the Jewish leaders could easily have gone to the tomb and produced Jesus' body to prove he didn't rise from the dead. But they couldn't because there was no body in the tomb.[1]

Some might say, "Maybe someone stole the body. Maybe the disciples snuck in, knocked out the guards and made off with Jesus' body and then claimed he had risen from the dead."

But they'd be wrong too. Dr Lennox points out that grave robbing was a very serious crime in the ancient world. If the Jewish leaders had any evidence that the disciples or anyone else had stolen Jesus' body, they could have hunted them down and arrested them. However, none of Jesus' followers was arrested for grave robbing.[2]

And if the resurrection of Jesus was all just a hoax, why did so many early Christians, including his own disciples, allow themselves to be tortured and put to death for claiming Jesus had risen? Would you let yourself be put to death for something you knew wasn't really true?

This extra evidence all backs up what the Bible says is true – Jesus is risen!

Did you know...

Did you know that one of the men who went to prison for being involved in the famous Watergate Scandal in the United States in the 1970's, Chuck Colson, came to believe that Jesus died for his sins and rose again? Colson worked for U.S. President Richard Nixon and, along with others, tried to keep secret that they had stolen documents in what became known as the 'Watergate Scandal'. After three weeks, Colson and the others told the truth and went to prison. Later, Colson said that it was this event that made him realise that Jesus must have risen from the dead. In one of his books, Colson wrote:

"I know the resurrection is a fact, and Watergate proved it to me. How? Because 12 men testified, they had seen Jesus raised from the dead, then they proclaimed that truth for 40 years, never once denying it. Every one was beaten, tortured, stoned, and put in prison. They would not have endured that if it weren't true. Watergate embroiled 12 of the most powerful men in the world, and they couldn't keep a lie for three weeks. You're telling me 12 apostles could keep a lie for 40 years? Absolutely impossible."[3]

- 7 -
Why can't I see you, God?

It's a good question. Why can't we see God?

The Bible tells us that God is not a human with flesh and blood like us, but that He is spirit. In the Gospel of John chapter 4 verse 24, Jesus tells a woman who doesn't know much about God that "God is spirit, and His worshippers must worship in the Spirit and in truth."

It's a bit like looking at the wind. We can't actually see wind, but we can feel its presence and we can see what happens when the wind blows through the trees.

God is spirit and therefore cannot be seen with a human eye. Yet by the Holy Spirit we can feel close to Him, and we can see all the good things He does in our lives and in the lives of others.

It's actually a good thing that God does hide His full glory from us. In the Old Testament book of Exodus, God tells His prophet Moses that he could not even handle catching a glimpse of God's face: "you cannot see my face, for man shall not see me and live."

And yet God was kind to Moses. God passed by Moses, covering Moses' eyes, but then, just for a moment, God allowed Moses to see His back as He passed.

The book of Exodus goes on to say that when Moses went back to the waiting Israelites, having seen just a tiny smidge of God's glory, his face shone so brightly, the people were afraid to go near him!

Importantly, even though God is invisible spirit, He became human in Jesus to reveal Himself to us. This means God also understands what it's like to be a human. Not just because He created us, but because He sent His Son, Jesus, down to earth to become a human, to live a human life and to die a human death.

What's awesome is that even though Jesus died as a human, God raised Him to new life to reign as King and as a wonderful sign of what awaits us if we believe and follow him.

Did you know...

Did you know that in the Old Testament, on one special day of the year, the High Priest of God's people was able to get physically closer to God than any other person? He was to enter a sacred room in the temple called the Most Holy Place which sat behind an enormous, thick curtain. The High Priest would then present a sacrifice to God for the sins of all the people. Only the High Priest could enter and only on that day of the year. If anyone entered on any other day, they would instantly die!

You know what? At the moment Jesus died, that huge curtain in the temple that separated God from His people ripped in half from top to bottom. This was a sign that through Jesus' sacrifice we can all stand in the presence of our Heavenly Father. How awesome!

- 8 -
Hey God, can you really do anything?

The Bible tells us that God is all powerful. That means there is nothing beyond His power to do. Remember, this is the God who called light, life, the universe, and everything into existence by simply speaking!

God can do anything, anywhere in heaven and on earth and throughout the universe at any moment.

In the Old Testament; the prophet Jeremiah wrote in the book of Jeremiah chapter 32 verse 17, "Ah, Lord GOD! It is you who have made the heavens and the earth by your great power and by your outstretched arm! Nothing is too hard for you."

That's right. Nothing is impossible for God.

But if nothing is impossible for God, does that mean God is able to do bad things or 'sin' like we do, if He wanted to?

What the Bible tells us is that God is not the author of evil and that God cannot be tempted to do evil. That's because sin and evil are simply not part of who God is.

In Jesus' disciple John's first letter, 1 John chapter 1 verse 5 the writer says, "God is light, and in Him there is no darkness at all."

In the book of James, also written by one of Jesus' disciples, chapter 1 verse 13, the writer says, "When tempted, no one should say, 'God is tempting me.' For God cannot be tempted by evil, nor does He tempt anyone;"

So, whether or not God has the 'ability' to sin doesn't even really matter. In God there is no sin. None at all.

Did you know...

Did you know that in the Old Testament David, who would one day be King of Israel, was absolutely convinced God could do anything? So much so, that when he was still a boy, he chose to fight a 10-foot-tall monster-of-a-man called Goliath. You see, David was angry that none of the soldiers in the army of God's people would fight Goliath.

David took only a sling – like a sling shot – and five stones. No spear, no armour, no sword. With his first stone, he cracked Goliath right between the eyes and the giant crashed to the ground, dead. That day, everyone knew there was nothing God could not do!

- 9 -
Hey God, how do I talk to you?

It's a great question. The simple answer is that we talk to God through prayer. Prayer is a conversation with God using words that come from your heart.

But how should we pray? What do we talk to God about?

Did you know that Jesus' own followers wanted to know the same thing? So, in the Gospel of Luke they ask Jesus, "Lord, teach us to pray."

Jesus told them how to pray to God in what has become known as the Lord's Prayer.

From verse 2 to verse 4 in the same chapter of Luke, it reads:

"He said to them, 'When you pray, say:

'Father, hallowed be your name, your kingdom come. Give us each day our daily bread.

Forgive us our sins, for we also forgive everyone who sins against us. And lead us not into temptation.'"

The first thing Jesus teaches them is that we can call God our 'Father'. In the language Jesus spoke, the actual word is 'Abba' which is a very personal word, like the name a child has for their dad. God wants us to know we are His children and for us to come into His presence, confident of His love for us. Isn't that amazing?

Jesus then taught his disciples to pray 'hallowed be your name.' That means to honour God as being perfectly holy and to try to live our lives as His holy precious children.

'Your kingdom come,' is praying that the truth of Jesus and the fact that he is God's chosen King should spread over the entire world. You and I can pray that today; that more and more people will come to believe in Jesus.

Jesus then teaches his followers to pray that God's 'will' be done in our lives and in the world around us. Jesus prayed this on the very last night before he died on the cross. Even though he didn't want to go through the pain of death, Jesus said to his Father God, "Not my will but yours be done".

We're also encouraged to ask for the things we need. That's what it means when Jesus prays "Give us each day our daily bread" in verse 3. God loves to give His children good things and He knows what we need before we ask.

An awesome part of the way Jesus taught us to pray is that it shows that we can directly ask God to forgive us for our sins. You see, because Jesus took our punishment, there is nothing separating us from God.

Even when we do bad things now, we can go directly to God and say, 'I'm sorry' and God says He will always forgive us. In the book of Romans chapter 8 verse 1 we're told "Therefore, there is now no condemnation for those who are in Christ Jesus."

Jesus also taught that we should pray that God will help us to show the same grace and forgiveness He shows to us to people who wrong us, especially when we don't feel like it.

Jesus then encourages his followers to call on God for protection; that He would hold firmly to our hand and help us not to be led astray when faced with temptation.

Temptation is the desire to do things that might feel good at first, but that we know in our hearts don't make God happy. It can be tough to resist. Even Jesus was tempted by the devil! That's why we pray that God will lead us away from temptation.

In all this, Jesus was teaching his disciples that there is so much we can talk to God about. Jesus talked to God when he was afraid, when he was joyful, when he was alone and when he was with his friends.

You can talk to God anytime, anywhere about anything and He will hear you because He cares about YOU!

Did you know...

Did you know that sometimes when we don't even know what to pray, God still hears us and knows what our hearts need? In Romans chapter 8 verse 26, we're told that "...the Spirit helps us in our weakness. We do not know what we ought to pray for, but the Spirit himself intercedes for us through wordless groans." The presence of God's Holy Spirit within us helps us draw near to Him.

- 10 -
How can I be sure you love me, God?

Imagine there's a kid at school who you've been really mean to. Like, really, really mean and you've been doing it all year. Sometimes you've even made this person cry. Now, imagine at the end of the year this kid is handing out big bags of Christmas candy to all the kids in your class. You know you're definitely not going to get one because you've been so horrible to this person all year.

Then to your surprise, the kid walks over and hands you a huge bag of candy. 'Merry Christmas!' they say. Wow. You didn't deserve any sort of gift at all and yet this other kid graciously gave you one.

That's kind of how we know how much God loves us.

We deserve death but God gives us eternal life.

You see, when Adam and Eve disobeyed God way back in the beginning, sin entered the world. Since then, sin stains each of us right from the moment we are born.

This stain of sin separated us from God and there was no way we could ever make things right. We deserved to pay the penalty for sin, which is death and separation from God forever.

But God loved us so much that He chose to have Jesus take that punishment for us. Paul tells us this in the book of Romans chapter 5 verse 8, "But God proves His own love for us in that while we were still sinners, Christ died for us!"

And even better, He made us His adopted children and one day we'll go home to be with our Father in His wonderful kingdom forever.

But what about when we still do bad stuff here and now? Will that make God stop loving us? No way! Jesus told a story to show us how much God loves us now, and how He forgives us when we're sorry.

The story can be found in the Gospel of Luke and is about a son who took his share of his inheritance from his dad and ran off to spend it on himself. He lived a wild life for a time, full of parties and selfish living. When the money ran out, he found himself taking work feeding pigs in the mud and was starving hungry.

He thought if he apologised to his dad, maybe his dad would take him back as a servant. At least that would be better than living in the mud with the pigs. So, he set off on the long journey back to his family home.

At last, the son saw his dad's house in the distance. Yet, while he was still a long way off, his dad ran to him. He wrapped him in the biggest bear-hug ever and kissed him on the head over and over. He then held a huge celebration because his son who was lost had been found.

Jesus used this story to show how great God's love is for us, and how completely He forgives us when we're sorry. Isn't that fantastic?

Did you know...

Did you know that Jesus predicted that one of his closest followers would betray him? In the Gospel of Matthew, Jesus told Peter that before the rooster crowed on the morning Jesus was to be put to death, Peter would deny he ever knew Jesus, not once but three times. And that's exactly what happened. But guess what? When Jesus had risen from the dead, he gave Peter the opportunity to say how much he loved Jesus, not once, but three times! Once for every time he'd denied Jesus, Jesus showed Peter how much he loved him.

- 11 -
Dear God, if you love us, why do bad and sad things still happen?

Imagine the most perfect apple you've ever seen. It's big, ripe and looks delicious. But when you cut open this beautiful looking apple, you realise a worm has eaten its way inside, leaving it horrible and rotten.

That's like what happened to our world. In Genesis, the first book of the Bible, we're told that God created the world and said it was 'very good'. Everything was just right. The weather was fantastic, the animals were friendly, and there was nothing bad or wrong. The first people He created, Adam and Eve, had everything they could want.

Then sin crept into this 'very good' world. Satan tempted Adam and Eve, lying to them, convincing them they didn't need God and even that they could be just like God. Adam and Eve chose to rebel against their loving God.

As a result, the world we now live in is rotten, just like that wormy apple. While good things happen all the time, bad things sometimes happen right alongside them. Sometimes bad things happen to really good people, even people we love. Sometimes they happen to us and it feels like our heart will break.

But here's the good news. When bad things happen, it doesn't mean God has forgotten us. It just means the world is broken. In fact, God promises to walk beside and comfort us during the hard times.

In the book of 2 Corinthians chapter 1 verses 3 and 4 the Apostle Paul writes, "Praise be to the God and Father of our Lord Jesus Christ, the Father of compassion and the God of all comfort, who comforts us in all our troubles, so that we can comfort those in any trouble with the comfort we ourselves receive from God."

Even better, because Jesus conquered sin and death by rising from the grave, one day all the brokenness of the world will be done away with.

There will be a new heaven and a new earth. In fact, in the book of Revelation chapter 21 verse 4 tells us that God Himself will "... wipe away every tear from their eyes. There will be no more death or mourning or crying or pain for the old order of things has passed away."

That's the future we have to look forward to!

Did you know...

Did you know that the Bible doesn't actually say Satan tempted Eve with an apple? The humble apple has always been pictured as the fruit that Adam and Eve tasted, choosing to disobey God. However, the Bible doesn't actually tell us what sort of fruit grew on that one special tree that Adam and Eve were told not to eat from. Just that it looked 'good for food' and 'pleasing to the eye'. We have no real idea what kind of fruit it was. So let's give the poor old apple a break!

- 12 -
Um, God, what if I'm scared of dying?

It's pretty normal to be scared of dying. It's hard-wired into our brains, and indeed into the brains of most living things.

Guess what? You're in good company. The Bible tells us that on the night before Jesus was put to death on the cross, he was so anxious that he prayed to his Father and asked if there was any way to take away the death he faced. We're also told that despite his anxiety, Jesus wanted to do what God wanted and trusted in his Father's great plan. God comforted Jesus in his time of anxiety, sending two angels to stand by him and strengthen him.

Jesus's disciples experienced fear of death as well.

In the Gospels of Matthew and Mark, we're told that on one occasion Jesus and his disciples were in a boat on a huge lake. While Jesus was asleep in the boat, a massive storm suddenly whipped up with massive waves and terrible winds.

The Bible tells us that his disciples became so afraid that they woke Jesus and said to him, "Lord, save us! We're going to drown!"

Jesus calmly stood and told the wind and waves to be still, and they obeyed.

Jesus asked his disciples "Why are you so afraid?"

It's a strange question because clearly powerful wind and gigantic waves that can kill a person are worth being afraid of!

Jesus wasn't talking about the wind and waves. He was talking about being afraid of death itself. Jesus was telling his disciples that he was the reason that no one should be afraid of death if God is with them.

You see, while the act of dying can be scary, we no longer need to be worried about death or what happens to us when we die, if we belong to Jesus.

In the Apostle Paul's letter found in 1 Corinthians chapter 15 verse 55, he writes that because of Jesus, death has no power anymore:

"Where, O death, is your victory?

Where, O death, is your sting?"

If you believe in Jesus, death is no longer the end. Rather it's the beginning of your eternal life in God's forever kingdom where the Bible tells us there will be no more crying, no more fear and most importantly no more death.

Did you know...

Did you know that in the Bible, God taps us on the shoulder to remind us not to be afraid? Well, sort of. In the book of Deuteronomy, chapter 31 verse 6, God tells us "Be strong and courageous. Do not be afraid or terrified because of them, for the Lord your God goes with you; he will never leave you nor forsake you." Then later in the book of Joshua chapter 1 verse 9, God gives us a little nudge to remind us of what we were told, "Have I not commanded you? Be strong and courageous. Do not be afraid; do not be discouraged, for the Lord your God will be with you wherever you go." God knows that sometimes we need reminding that He is always with us wherever we go.

- 13 -
So, God, why should I obey you?

We obey God because He is the one who saved us by sending Jesus to take the penalty for our sin. Sin had trapped us so tight that, as the Apostle Paul tells us in Romans chapter 6, we were like slaves and that it was God who set us free. In verse 17 of Romans chapter 6, it says: "But thanks be to God that, though you used to be slaves to sin, you have come to obey from your heart the pattern of teaching that has now claimed your allegiance. You have been set free from sin and have become slaves to righteousness."

We also obey God because it's a way of showing how grateful we are for what He has done for us. We obey God because we really do want to follow Jesus and have him be King in our lives.

And we obey God because we love Him. In the book of 1 John chapter 4 verse 16, Jesus' disciple John writes: 'God is love. Whoever lives in love lives in God, and God in them." John goes on to write in verses 19 and 20: "We love because he first loved us. Whoever claims to love God yet hates a brother or sister is a liar. For whoever does not love their brother and sister, whom they have seen, cannot love God, whom they have not seen."

Another reason we obey God is because we trust that He knows what's best for us. When we disobey God we can hurt our relationship with Him, just like the son who ran away from his dad in the Gospel of Luke chapter 15. When we disobey God, we can also hurt those around us like our parents, our brothers and sisters, our friends and even ourselves. You see, God wants us to obey Him because He really cares for us and knows what's best for us.

In the book of Proverbs chapter 3 verses 5 and 6 it says: "Trust in the LORD with all your heart and lean not on your own understanding; in all your ways submit to Him, and He will make your paths straight."

True blessing can be found in obeying God.

Did you know...

Did you know that carpenters have a saying, 'measure twice, cut once.' What that means is it's better to do things the right way, than to 'cut corners' and make a mistake which can be painful and costly to fix. Obeying God is kind of like that. God loves and cares for us and knows what's best for our lives. We can find blessing in doing things God's way. When we disobey God, He will always forgive us when we're sorry, but sometimes there can still be pain in fixing our mistake!

- 14 -
Hey God, what should I say to my friends who don't believe you are real?

One of the best things we can do for our friends is be a good listener. Perhaps it might be an idea to ask them why they don't believe God is real, and what they believe instead.

When someone feels like you've really listened to what they have to say, they're often more willing to listen to what you believe and why. That's why we also need to be prepared to tell our friends what we believe about God and His son, Jesus.

Jesus' disciple Peter wrote to fellow Christians about this in a letter recorded in the Bible. In 1 Peter chapter 3 verse 15, Peter tells Christians: "Always be prepared to give an answer to everyone who asks you to give the reason for the hope that you have. But do this with gentleness and respect..."

A good way to 'be prepared' is to practise saying out loud, maybe in the quietness of your own room, why you DO believe in God and His Son Jesus. Keep it simple and talk about the things that help you know God is real. Maybe ask your parents for some help.

Maybe you could talk about the things you've learned in this book – who God is; the evidence that He created the world; the accuracy and truth of the Bible; the fact that Jesus was a real person who lived and was killed on the cross; and the evidence that he rose from the dead and appeared to many people. Most importantly, you could tell them what that means for us and how we can be part of God's family forever! You could also invite your friends to church or kids' church or your youth group. This can be tough to do sometimes, but it might surprise you how many times your friends will say 'yes'.

And most of all, pray for your friends. Pray that God will open their eyes and that they will see that Jesus Christ is their King and their friend. That he died and rose again for them, so that they would be counted as his, and one day, be with him in heaven forever.

Did you know...

Did you know that there was once a famous journalist who wrote for the Chicago Tribune named Lee Strobel, who set out to prove God wasn't real? You see, he was so upset when his wife told him she'd decided to follow Jesus that he decided to write a book proving that Jesus was NOT the Son of God and that Christianity was not true. Lee looked at all the evidence and asked Christian leaders really tough questions. And when he was finished, guess what happened? Lee Strobel gave his life to Jesus as well! He found that all the evidence he'd collected really did point to a risen Jesus who was his King and friend.[1] So why not your friends too?

Conclusion

I hope this book has helped with some of your big questions for God. Maybe it will help you give answers to your friends and family when they ask questions about who God is and why He sent Jesus.

If you take one thing away from reading this book, I pray it's this: God, who created everything, wanted to make you His adopted child so much, that He sent Jesus, His only Son, to take your place and pay the penalty for your sin. By faith in Jesus, you are made right with God forever and can know how deeply God loves you now and always. One day, Jesus will return to make you a part of God's wonderful new kingdom forever. What great news!

This may be the first time you've thought about God, His Son Jesus, and the Bible. If you've decided you want to be part of God's forever family and have Jesus as your King and your friend, that's terrific!

You can tell God that by praying this short prayer. It's a very special moment between you and Jesus: "Dear Jesus, I believe you were a real person and that you are God's Son. I believe that you died on the cross to save me and that you rose again, conquering death for all time. Please forgive me for my sin and for living my life my own way. Now, I want you to be my king, and I want to be part of God's family, now and forever. Amen."

If you prayed that prayer from your heart, you are now part of God's family. He is your loving Father, who you can talk to anytime, thanks to what Jesus did for you.

The next step is to tell someone you trust and you know is also a Christian, that you prayed this prayer. This could be your parents, your grandparents, your Sunday school teacher or maybe even the person that gave you this book. They can pray for you and help you find ways to learn more about what it means to follow Jesus.

Most of all, trust Jesus. He knows you and loves you. He will be with you always.

Brad R. Emery

References

Biblical Text – Holy Bible, New International Version®, NIV® Copyright ©1973, 1978, 1984, 2011 by Biblica, Inc.® Used by permission. All rights reserved worldwide.

Hey God, who are you really?
1. http://www.kanyini.com/what-is-kanyini.html - Kanyini - A film by Melanie Hogan – As told by Bob Randall, a "Tjilpi" (special teaching uncle) of the Yankunytjatjara Nation – with thanks to Pastor Ray Minniecon, Scarred Tree Ministries, St. John's Anglican Church, Glebe NSW.

God, did you really create Australia, the world and everything?
1. https://www.nytimes.com/1991/03/12/science/sizing-up-the-cosmos-an-astronomer-s-quest.html
2. https://www.pewforum.org/2009/11/05/scientists-and-belief/
3. https://www.sfgate.com/news/article/FINDING-MY-RELIGION-Leader-of-the-Human-Genome-3299361.php

Dear God, how can I be sure the Bible is true and accurate?
1. John C. Lennox, Gunning for God. Why the new atheists are missing the target, Lion Books 2011, p. 192-193
2. McDowell S, "Is the New Testament Reliable?", in Decision The Evangelical Voice for Today, April 2015, Billy Graham Evangelical Association https://decisionmagazine.com/new-testament-reliable/#
3. McDowell, Josh, and Sean McDowell. Evidence That Demands a Verdict: Life-Changing Truth for a Skeptical World, Authentic 2017, p. 59
4. McDowell S, "Is the New Testament Reliable?", in Decision The Evangelical Voice for Today, April 2015, Billy Graham Evangelical Association
5. McDowell S, "Is the New Testament Reliable?", in Decision The Evangelical Voice for Today, April 2015, Billy Graham Evangelical Association

Excuse me God, was Jesus just make believe or was he a real person?
1. https://www.bethinking.org/jesus/ancient-evidence-for-jesus-from-non-christian-sources
2. E.P. Sanders, The Historical Figure of Jesus, Penguin Books 1993, p.11
3. Christopher Tuckett, "Sources and Methods", in The Cambridge Companion to Jesus, ed. Markus Bockmuehl, Cambridge, Cambridge University Press, 2001, p. 124
4. Gerd Theissen and Annette Merz, The Historical Jesus: a comprehensive guide, Minneapolis, Fortress Press, 1998, pp. 93-94

Dear God, did Jesus really rise from the dead?
1. John C. Lennox, Gunning for God. Why the new atheists are missing the target, Lion Books 2011, p. 206-207
2. John C. Lennox, Gunning for God. Why the new atheists are missing the target, Lion Books 2011, p. 206-207
3. Charles Colson, https://www.youtube.com/watch?v=ZZ5fm1uPCzs

About the author

Brad Emery grew up with two heroes: his dad, the Reverend John Emery, who travelled to some of the most dangerous corners of the globe to teach people about Jesus; and his mum, Robyn, who was the glue that held their family together.

Growing up in a Christian home, Brad was lucky to have parents who were both very knowledgeable, and who also possessed an extensive library to help answer his many questions about God, His Son and the 'whys and wherefores' of the world around us.

However, when Brad became a parent himself, he realised that not all Christian parents had such resources at their disposal. Brad also found it a struggle to find Christian literature designed to provide primary school aged children with Biblical answers to some of the common questions that arise out of the Bible. Helping to provide answers to questions about God, His world and His amazing plan to reconcile us to Himself has never been more important and with the support of close friends, Brad decided to write "Hey God, can I ask you something?".

Brad is a professional writer who brings more than two decades of writing experience in the fields of media relations, industry, and politics to his personal writing projects. Brad is a contracted writer with The Sydney Morning Herald and over the last two decades, has had dozens of articles published in Christian publications such as Eternity and Southern Cross, as well as secular publications such as The Huffington Post, 10Daily and Investor Weekly.

Brad lives in Sydney with his wife Renee and their daughter Willow. They attend The Bridge Church, Neutral Bay NSW, Australia.

www.ingramcontent.com/pod-product-compliance
Lightning Source LLC
Chambersburg PA
CBRC091958300426
44109CB00007BA/164